Super Emotions!

A Book for Children with AD/HD

by Lionel Lowry IV

To Lee, Lillie, Laander, Tim, my parents, and all of my family, and friends along the way,

Keep laughing - *Lionel*

Super Emotions!
A Book for Children with AD/HD
Copyright © 2013 by Lionel Lowry IV

All rights reserved.

Written by Lionel Lowry IV
Cover and book design by Lionel Lowry IV

Lionel Lowry IV
www.SuperEmotions.com

Super Emotions!

A Book for Children with AD/HD

by

Lionel Lowry IV

This book belongs to ...

_____

Breathe in.

Breathe out.

Relax.

Good morning.

So they say you have AD/HD,

So what does this mean, my friend?

This means you have Super Emotions,

And you need to learn to control them.

Your emotions give you power,

Power to dream and think, and play.

Learn to use them correctly,

And you'll be A-Okay.

When you are happy, you may be very, very happy,

When you are sad, you may be oh so very sad,

When you are excited, you may be extremely excited,

And when you are angry, you may be incredibly MAD!

Your parents and your doctors

Will help show you what to do.

They will ask lots of questions and give you tests,

They will work hard to help you.

Sometimes you will feel so happy,

You'll want to jump and scream, and shout.

Make sure that it's appropriate where you are,

You don't want to get thrown out.

Sometimes you will feel so sad,

Like everything is bleak and bad.

Just remember how much your family loves you,

Good feelings will come back, and you'll feel great and glad.

There are many things you can try,

When your feelings get to you.

Two of them are exercise and art,

Try them and they will help you through.

Paint, draw, dance,

Run, skip, and swim,

Let your Super Emotions flow,

And you will start to feel better again.

You have the Super Powers,

To help your Super Self calm down.

Believe in yourself and try every day,

You are a Super Hero, be proud!

Super Hero, you are loved,

Every part of you is fantastic.

Your Super Emotions make you special,

Just help them be less drastic.

It's time to rest your Super Emotions,

And let peace fill your soul.

Let yourself be calm and relaxed,

And let your Super Self take control.

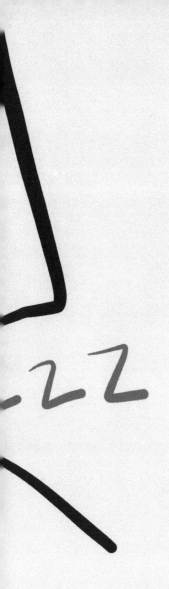

Breathe in.

Breathe out.

Relax.

Good night.

shhhh... the end

Friends,

If you like this Super Emotions! book, and think it might help others,
please ask them to visit www.SuperEmotions.com

We are a group of youth-minded people dedicated to enriching lives and
empowering children. We appreciate your support.

Thank you!

Sincerely,

Lionel

CPSIA information can be obtained
at www.ICGtesting.com
Printed in the USA
LVHW071913211121
704026LV00002B/85